A MUST READ!

The Book within A Book

PALMETTO
P U B L I S H I N G
Charleston, SC
www.PalmettoPublishing.com

Copyright © 2024 by Debra Steele

All rights reserved

No portion of this book may be reproduced, stored in a retrieval system, or transmitted in any form by any means–electronic, mechanical, photocopy, recording, or other–except for brief quotations in printed reviews, without prior permission of the author.

Paperback ISBN: 979-8-8229-3888-5
eBook ISBN: 979-8-8229-3889-2

The Book within A Book

A MEMOIR AND A CLEAR VISION

DEBRA STEELE

*I would like to dedicate this book to my great grandfather
Cesare Rastellini born in Italy 1885.
He bravely began our familiar history here in America!*

*I also dedicate this book to my beautiful Aunt Marie
She's played a huge part in the birth of this book
with her timeless memories!*

*I also dedicate this book to my adoring son Thomas.
He has been my life's inspiration from the very first breath he took.
He lovingly and proudly has and continues to embrace his
Italiano roots.*

Forever in my heart!

CONTENTS

Introduction · 1
Chapter 1 Before My Birth · 3
Chapter 2 Sweet Lorraine · 8
Chapter 3 Health · 14
Chapter 4 Family · 18
Chapter 5 Strength · 22
Chapter 6 Spiritual Guidance · 25
About the Author · 34

INTRODUCTION

Some may find it odd when I say I didn't write my book, that my book wrote me.

Suddenly I was woken up in the middle of the night. As words were literally pouring into my mind, as though I had a water faucet running on full blast. I couldn't turn it off. The very next morning, I decided to put these thoughts on paper, hence the birth of *The Book within a Book*.

In this book I will cover love, faith, health, friendship, family, and strength! But most of all, it will uncover a much higher spirit with divine guidance. My wish is this book inspires everyone who embraces it to have hope and most importantly, life's answers.

Thank you for choosing my book for your read!

I'm very grateful!

TERAMO FAMILY

RASTELLINI FAMILY

Chapter 1

BEFORE MY BIRTH

It all started February 1904 when my great grandfather Cesare Rastellini migrated from Sant' Omero Teramo, Italy to America. The last place he resided in before boarding the ship out of Naples, Italy, at age nineteen to Ellis Island in 1904 was 24 Case Alte Sant' Omero Teramo, Italy. Translate 24 High St. Sant' Omero Teramo, Italy, located in the Abruzzo region of eastern Italy. Cesare and wife Annie's second child of thirteen would turn out to be my grandfather Fioravanti (Fio). My grandmother Marie Lapore was born the third child of four in her family. Together my grandparents created a large loving Italian family of nine, which grew from there. Now fast forward to the year 1941 in Somerville, Massachusetts, my father had already been born the sixth child of nine, and as a little boy he would discover his hidden talent in music simply by ear at a very early age of just seven. As it is told, my father would nestle into the family's living room sofa, while lying an acoustic guitar across his sweet little lap—if you can imagine! Full-grown, my father stood a whopping five feet, two inches tall and just 135 pounds, so a sweet little lap at age seven is an understatement at best, the guitar was much bigger than him!

The traditional manner in which the guitar was to be played did not interest my father in the least little bit during his early years, and it wasn't until much later in life did he journey on to other musical instruments, such as the electric guitar and bass guitar—he even dabbled a bit in drums—but his true *love* would turn out to be the steel guitar, otherwise known as the Hawaiian guitar. I understand why; this instrument exerts the most beautiful sounds your ears will ever hear, which would inspire anyone with musical aspirations. And because of this, my father had such an interest in writing and composing music from this day forward. He joined a band at the age of seventeen and found themselves playing music at a local bar while secretly under the drinking age of eighteen. But no one questioned him. As an Italian he was blessed with a full head of beautiful hair, not to mention a five o'clock shadow in his early teens, so on stage playing music, acting and looking the part came with ease and felt very natural to him, including the audience.

As he grew older into his later teens, he was especially fond of country music and of course all music of the '50s. Who doesn't love '50s music? Even now in 2023, we all embrace the music of those days.

On my father's music journey, he finally got his chance to compose and produce his long-awaited dream, which would turn out to be his first and *only* album, which came to be endorsed by Freddie Hart, a well-known country singer of his time. My father even traveled the music circuit from Idaho to Wichita falls, Wyoming, California, and Florida. As he relocated during his music years, band names would come and go, but the one most important name that stuck with him was George Steele, connected to his deep-rooted love of the steel guitar. This is where I come in. Like my father, I, too, chose to embrace the name "Debra Steele" as my book signature, channeling my dear father on my book journey.

Going back to my large Italian side of my family: our dear "Noni," short for "Mamma Non," which is translated Grandma, was an orphan at age three herself, so all babies (including the seven she gave birth to later in life and even her eighth baby who she lost, Ruth) were near and dear to her heart. For her, taking in a stranger here and there was totally natural and heartwarming, to say the least, much like her love of cooking. She always welcomed everyone into her home with loving open arms, ready to feed them one of her delicious Italian meals. As the Italians would say, "*mangia, mangia,*" which translates as "*eat, eat,*" and boy could she cook like no other!

On this one magical day, a gift showed up at her door; as she would tell it, no doubt from the heavens above. Deep in her heart and soul, she felt that she had been blessed with a beautiful baby boy, especially after losing baby Ruth. Gosh, the Lord was good to her this day, as he very well knew she harbored such amazing motherly skills, which clearly explained him delivering her such happiness. But little did she know, she would soon be gifted with yet another little boy, who would turn out to be her baby's brother. In that very moment, she felt God had chosen her for those precious little bundles of pure joy. As it turned out, one of the band members in the band with my father, Tommy Wayne, had an extra marital affair with one of the local bar gals. In fact, word be told that, as she was giving birth to her first son, she would soon learn that the band member's wife was down that very hall giving birth at the same time as well. What a small world it was! The Lord does work in a very mysterious way, doesn't he? We'll touch base on this subject again later in this book.

It wouldn't be until approximately two or three years later our Noni would experience her heart being ripped from the very chest that housed her enormous heart-felt love for those two boys. She found herself facing the challenge of a lifetime. She must give up one of those babies. The thought of this would become unimaginable for her as well as extremely devastating. This unthinkable choice would turn out to be so heart-wrenching for her. Now faced with one of the toughest decisions of her lifetime, which one could she live without? Because in her world, neither! This devastating news was well after she had given her time and unconditional love as mothers do. Her love was shared with both, 100 percent equally, for months, even years, compiling endless hours of loving care in mothering these babies, day after day, night after night, year after year, only to have the biological mother show up on her doorstep to reclaim one of them. She told Noni that she was sorry, but she had promised one of the boys to another dear friend of hers. You could only imagine how hard this was on her. As Noni's eyes filled with tears and her heart pounded in her chest, there was absolutely nothing she could do!

There was no documentation giving Noni sole custody. She was even scared as to not upset the boy's mother by any means of a fight or any type of rebellion. She still had the other baby in her arms and did not want to jeopardize the loss of him too. As she watched through her tears, her beloved little Tommy, the younger of the two, was taken from her loving arms forever. This devastating move by the boy's mother would prove to impact Noni's life like nothing else.

She went on to cry for months on end due to the loss of the baby, Tommy. But what I think the deeper-rooted problem was for her was in that moment was wondering, *will baby Tommy continue to receive the same love and care she was able to provide him,* and *will it be in the same manner he had come to know?* For her, not knowing was a huge punch to the gut. Still, she had to compose herself because the brother needed her desperately. Her goal became to legally adopt baby Wayne. She could not risk her motherly connection, and tragedy could not disrupt her loving home again. But to secure this goal, she would find herself fighting an uphill battle. Unfortunately at that time, the state of Massachusetts had a cap on the age limit of persons wanting to adopt. The challenge was that both Noni and Grampy Fio were in their fifties; this could prevent them from reaching their goal, at least for the time being, but she would not lose focus on the goal.

We'll touch base on this again later in the story.

Meanwhile, Noni's life would take yet another turn, involving another child's journey. This journey was called "Sweet Lorraine." Which will now bring this story even closer to home and into our next chapter.

Chapter 2
SWEET LORRAINE

As you may have guessed by now, Sweet Lorraine was my beautiful mother, my best friend, and my forever soul mother. She is also the main reason behind my inspiration to write this book, *Book within a Book*, which we will get to later in the book. First you must know that Noni ended up taking in my mother Lorraine at the age of twelve, just as she had done previously with the baby boys.

Don't get me wrong, nothing happened to my grandmother on my mother's side, whom we called "Nane." On the contrary, my French-Irish grandmother was a bit of a heavy port wine drinker most of her life, as well as a bit risqué for her times. She was even fluid in the French language, and who's not mesmerized when hearing such a beautiful language being spoken? If that's not a head-turning moment, imagine hearing this romantic language being spoken by a very beautiful woman.

THE BOOK WITHIN A BOOK

Nane was quite stunning. I know where my mother's beauty came from. Nane could have had anyone she wanted, yet somehow, she would find herself caught up in relationship with a married Catholic man, who would become my mother's biological father, Peter.

As it turned out, Nane and Peter both brought my mother Lorraine, then three years later, her brother Donald, into the world during their secretive relationship. Living this risqué type of lifestyle most often ends up in total devastation for all parties involved, and in this case, that very devastation hit home hard and unexpected. As my mother told the story: it was one Christmas day that changed my mother's life path forever. She could never get past that day. You see, in my mother's eyes, the sun rose and set on her beloved father Peter, unconditionally. As it is told, my mother was maybe ten at the time and had been giving that devastating news on Christmas day. Her father Peter and mother Sadie had pledged to end their relationship. Little did my mother know Peter *must* do this to save his marriage, but he vowed to stay in contact with my mother, and he kept his word. He owned a restaurant in the city of Boston, where they would secretly meet often to get caught up and to embrace one another. Gosh, they loved one another so much. How do I know this? She would bring my father's little sister Marie, my aunt, along with her on those visits. They were the best of friends and loved each other as sisters do. She could rely on my aunt to keep a good secret, and she did just that without question.

Here is where I mentioned earlier in the chapter that explains how Noni came to my mother's rescue at the age of twelve.

That devastating Christmas day when Nane was told by Peter the relationship was over seemed to have triggered an already heavy drinking grandmother to fall even deeper into the bottle. She had convinced herself over the years that their relationship would be forever and nothing could come between them, not even his marriage, so her receiving that devastating news on Christmas day, like my mother was damming with scares of pain for both Nane and my mom. We've all come to know that there are happy drinkers or not-so-happy drinkers. We would soon find out this devastating news would rear the head of the not-so-happy drinker! For these reasons, both Nane and my mother clashed terribly. My mom blamed Nane for that dreadful day, vowing never to forgive her. Nane eventually did find love, but not her true love. Peter had her heart.

Unbeknown to Nane, she had *no* idea my mother was keeping the biggest secret of all from her. That secret was that both she and my father had been seeing each other for some time. As time went on, he ended up giving her this sweet little beautiful gold promise ring shaped into a little bow. The bow sat nestled in a rim of gold with two ruby stones as bow ends. He knew rubies were my mother's favorite stone as well as her July birthstone. There sat a little clear stone separating the two bow ends, which made the bow stand out even more. Again, it was such a sweet little ring. This ring turned out to pack such a *huge* promise for both. Being where they were, twelve and thirteen at the time, promising themselves to one another made my father my mother's first and only boyfriend. He would turn out to be the one and only man she was to ever love unconditionally. He had her heart 100 percent and knew it.

On this one ugly day, apparently her mother, Sadie, had a drunken spell that excelled well over and above the tolerant levels for any type of conversation or discussions my mother felt she needed to have with her. As the story is told, it got downright ugly that day. You can only imagine how uncomfortable these two young kids—my mother and her brother Donald—were. In that volatile moment, my mom grabbed her younger brother Donald to protect him, to remove him from any danger that may have come from the ugliness. My mother always protected him like she was his little mother herself. She just adored him.

Her intentions were to head straight toward the door and get out as fast as they could to a safe place. My mom was a bit of spitfire herself, so fire mixed with fire could easily become explosive, to say the least. She grabbed her brother and the necessary clothing she felt needed should they be gone for days and headed toward the door. She knew right where to go, Noni's loving arms. That was the safest place for her and her little brother. Noni welcomed them with open arms and that awesome motherly protection they came to rely on from that very day. Noni would do just that, protect them with her entire being. Besides that, my Italian family absolutely loved and adored my mother dearly.

So when my Nane called Noni's home looking for my mom and her little brother, my grandpa Fio heard the call. He took that call and ripped into Nane for her verbal abuse and volatile actions toward my mother and Donald, vowing to provide my mom and her brother a roof over their heads for as long as they wanted and felt safe.

Back then, you didn't argue with an Italian man who wore the pants in the house. It just didn't happen, and you would be crazy to try. Let's just say, Nane did not pursue contact again, which was a smart move on her end. She got his message loud and clear.

As the years went by, looking at my mother and father in a whole new light. They were both in their late teens and forced to grow up fast. My father was living his dream, playing in the band nightly while working in a shoe shop during the day, all to make ends meet and contribute to the large household. He was always a hard worker his entire life, sometimes working two or three jobs.

They had built a solid, loving relationship and adored each other immensely. The next part of their relationship brought them to a much higher level, when they found out they were pregnant with their first child, who would turn out to be my big brother, George. My mother was just seventeen, giving birth to my brother in September of 1954. You see, I hadn't been thought of at that point yet!

I guess I would be that twinkle in my daddy's eye, waiting to come into the world when they least expected me. I would show my little face to the world approximately twenty-one months (about two years) later, and I won the heart of my daddy. I know this because my family would tell me all sorts of stories as young children that we would not have remembered as babies. We lived with my Italian side of the family for the first three to four years of our little lives. They had so many memorable moments to share with us as we grew older. The one most important story that stuck with me and had my full and unconditional attention during my life was this: I would hear my father come home after playing music during the wee hours of the morning, and I would stand right up in my crib all excited waiting to see him with open arms. They said this would have such a melting effect on him, as these special little moments between him and I would contribute toward building a bond of deep, pure, and innocent love between my father and I forever!

Many years later I ended up losing my dear father to liver cancer. He was just fifty-nine. I don't think I'll ever get over losing him, and to this very day, I continue to struggle with that loss. He sure was a very special daddy. We had such a deep loving bond that nothing other than death itself could penetrate. I miss him dearly without question. I find that for me to go on living with such a huge void is to continue praying and talking to my father always, vowing to never stop. It is very comforting.

Chapter 3

HEALTH

Going back years prior to the loss of my father in 1995, while growing up, we were a devout Catholic family. Mom always brought us to church but not just for Sunday service, which at that time, the entire service was in Latin, also we attended Saturday Catechism, as well as services every Wednesday. I went on to experience having my first Holy Communion and Confirmation, so it's safe to say we were an active family in and out of the church.

Remember Noni's goal to adopt? Well as it turns out, the state of California did *not* have an age limit cap when it came to adoption, unlike Massachusetts. So we all packed up the vehicles stuffed to the hilt, and we began the journey across the United States from Boston to California. I was just five years old when we left Boston, so it didn't matter to me where I lived. I was with my family and very content.

Finally, we had hopes of seeing Noni's dream of adoption possibly coming true. Even if this process would prove to take time, we were heading in the right direction. Noni felt that she could start to breathe. As one would say, we were starting to see the light at the end of her tunnel. Patience would end up paying off, no matter what, at that point.

Her goal of adoption would turn out to take a long time, even years, before Noni's dream came to fruition. However, our patience did finally pay off. By the time it was all said and done, her little boy was now a sixteen-year-old living in the state of California and going through the adoption process with the loving family that took him in as a newborn. That day would turn out to be one of the most important and memorable days of both Noni and Grampy Fio's lives, as they could now take a *huge* breath and start to relax.

They were on top of the world, their goal had finally been met, and of course, we joyfully celebrated that memorable day. Life was good.

All went well for several years living in our new surroundings. We found ourselves all grown up, starting families of our own. Babies making babies. We all got caught up in our busy lives and started to go our separate ways, until our Italian side of the family once again wanted to relocate. But this time for entirely different reasons. Grampy Fio was retiring, and they could sell their home in California and pay cash for their new home in Florida. That would make a big difference financially in their new Florida lifestyle. Over those challenging years, both Noni and Grampy Fio had gone through so much, and let's face it, they were not getting any younger as the years seemed to be flying by. Their idea of relocating to Florida, the Sunshine State, bolstered with warm seasons, paired with a slow pace of living, would turn out to be a really good fit for our aging family founders!

Noni struggles with arthritis in her knees, making it next to impossible for her to be on her feet for any length of time, but so far, Florida is the perfect move for them. They arrived in Florida to settle in the later part of the 1970s, which made the move easy because their first-born daughter, Anna, her husband George, and their two children had already been living there for quite some time. They were familiarized with the Florida lifestyle, and the "snowbirds" that are famously known to Florida.

Next to follow the relocation was their daughter Marie, who came to love Florida so much that she met with a local builder, and the start of her brand-new home began, all while living in an apartment. *Fun*! She ended up getting my parents to commit to relocating from California to Florida, convincing my father to fly out immediately to meet up with her builder. Not only did my parents meet with her builder, but I also met with them as well, and the building of *all* our homes was set in motion. Fortunately for me, at that time there was an empty lot right next door to my mother and father's lot. I jumped on it! Once again, we found ourselves packing up a large U-Haul truck, as well as the vehicle in tow, plus the vehicles both my brother George and I drove, overstuffed with all our belongings. Our cross-country journey began in April of 1978. By then, we were very experienced in relocation, so this was a breeze. We arrived in Florida just five days later. At that time, in 1978, I was a new mother myself. Along with our belongings was the most important cargo of all, my beautiful little boy, Thomas. He came to me on the sixteenth of April, 1976, the best day ever.

THE BOOK WITHIN A BOOK

I was excited for Noni and Thomas to meet. Noni had not had the chance to meet him yet.

Over the years Thomas would grow up to be a wonderful son and husband, full of such great family values, which pleases me immensely. Plus, in his journey he not only found his forever soulmate, but he also found one of the rarest soulmates of all. He found a perfect little angel, Kristi, which makes my heart warm. As both of our loving families blended, her mother Betty and father Johnny would claim Thomas as the son they never had, and I would claim Kristi as the daughter I never had. Like them, I just adore her and her loving, kind soul. We are all so lucky!

We try to embrace the special times to help overcome our sad times, and we do have our share.

As years passed, it turned out Noni needed as much family around her as possible because she and Grampy Fio's future would be cut short. Unbeknown to them, Fio's health had taken a bad turn, and he was diagnosed with lung cancer. They immediately began twenty-eight rounds of chemo, and within ten short days, he would pass. He was sixty-nine, just one year older than Noni. All attention turned to Noni. She struggled with weight issues, which have taken a toll on her heart and knees.

God love her. She stood four foot nine by five feet *wide*, and every inch of her was nothing short of pure, endless love and compassion for *all* she came to know and love.

We would soon be faced with the unthinkable, which I will go into the next chapter.

Chapter 4
FAMILY

With the stress of Noni being overweight for most of her life, it caused her to have an enlarged heart. It was concerning to us, to say the least, so we kept a good eye on her. She always had family around her, and that was most important to her.

She spent a great deal of her last days doing what she wanted, surfing from family to family, with whom she loved playing cards and board games till all hours of the night. She was a hoot! She was such an amazing soul. She was contagious, on steroids. We would all want her to be at our homes, almost bickering over her!

We became aware that her days were numbered. The doctors had given the family detailed medical information pertaining to her health issues and what we all needed to be aware of. At that point we all knew we could never leave her alone. This followed just two years after losing Grampy Fio.

Two and a half years after Grampy Fio's passing, we were faced with the inevitable. While Noni was sitting at my mother's kitchen table, as she did so many times, Mom was preparing lunch for all of us while Noni and I were engaged in family conversation. Suddenly there was a change in her expressions and her demeanor. I looked at her, waiting for her to answer me from across the table. She had my full attention in that moment, looking closely at her, still trying to get a response. I felt a deep gut punch. I knew this was not going to have a good outcome. I felt it from the depths of my stomach, as I could see right into her soul through her loving eyes.

I started to desperately try and help her any way I could, as my mother dialed 911 frantically. I felt help wouldn't make it in time to save her. We would be faced with witnessing her end-of-life journey. My thoughts became gospel in that very moment. Both my dear mother and I were witnessing our precious Noni silently slipping away before our very eyes. Our eyes filled with huge tears as we embraced one another tightly, hoping the medics working on her could pull off the biggest miracle of all. It felt as though they had worked on her for hours. As my stomach was in knots, my gut senses would turn out to be right. There was nothing they could do to save her. All our lives would change in that very moment.

I started praying, and in my prayer, I thanked God that he made sure she was surrounded by loving family and not alone. I would continue to thank God for not letting her suffer, while at the same time, giving me the strength to hold it together because at that point, I needed to be strong for my mother. She was a wreck! Noni was her second mom; they were extremely close. But little did I know this would *not* be the last time I was to see Noni again in this lifetime.

Back to that later in the book.

My mother's health was on a downward spiral too. I was concerned with what took place in her kitchen, which would turn out to be one of our darkest days. This day prompted thoughts: could it trigger deeper health issues within my own mother? I was scared my mother's poor failing health was in danger too.

When my mother was younger, in her early twenties, she experienced female issues such as irregular menstrual cycles. She had been prescribed birth control pills to help regulate her cycle, and they seemed to be working for her, so they thought. We would come to find out later, there should have been other avenues explored by her prescribing doctor. But we had all been taught to trust the doctors! Much to our surprise, the doctor prescribing them ignored all the tell-tale signs to *stop* the medication. From this miss, she developed several health issues, ultimately forcing her to undergo twenty-two major, life-threatening surgeries just to keep her alive. We were lucky to have her. We could have lost her at any given time with any one of those surgeries.

Suddenly we were noticing a pattern of bad health plaguing our family as we started to lose family members, one by one. And it didn't stop there!

After losing Noni, seven years later, in May of 1987, we would lose my beloved mother, sweet Lorraine. She was just forty-nine. It all stemmed back to the words "lucky to have had her," and we truly were, for as long as we did.

Tragedy in our family continued. We then lost Noni's son Joe at age fifty-two from a brain tumor, followed by her son Charlie, from a heart attack. Then her daughter Anna, from pancreatic cancer in 2000, followed by my father George at age fifty-nine, of liver cancer.

If that wasn't devastating enough, within the next two years, I would go on to lose not only my father at age fifty-nine, but I also lost my brother George at age forty-three, followed by my Nane at age eighty-three on my mother's July 21 birthday, well after my mom's passing.

It was more than enough for one family to handle. Finally, it seemed we were granted a much-needed break. Thank God!

But it was not over. We would, as a family, be plagued once again with more losses. Noni's other two sons passed, Billy and then Teddy, leaving our dearest Marie, age eighty-three, as the sole survivor of what once was our large Italian family that we had all come to lovingly embrace for all our lives. But at that point, I would take it. I wanted my aunt to live for many more years, for eternity, which would suit me just fine!

Chapter 5
STRENGTH

As life went on, we found ourselves repeating our ancestors' lives. We all began our own adult life journeys in finding our soulmates, having children of our own. As adults we found ourselves sharing precious memories to tell such stories as were told when we grew up. So yes, life did go on. I truly believe we never really get over our losses, we all just learn to accept them as a way of life.

Today we live in a very busy world, so family gatherings are few and far between, yet we all still feel that strong family bond deep within. All of Noni's children have had children of their own, even some of their children have had children of their own. So, it's nice to know the family blood goes on. Most of us have met our soulmates and have already spent countless years with them committed to ever-after love.

This I know makes Noni happy. She is still here spiritually with us, often visiting her daughter Marie in her dreams. We know about our dreams now, don't we? Family is strength, and because of family, we are a strong bunch. We're able to face any situation a family is faced with and seem to grow stronger by the minute.

As for my situation, much later in life, both my husband of thirty-two years, Erik, and I were plagued with serious health issues as well. But through our issues I can honestly say, he has been my boulder, and I, his rock. Together, our strength is untouchable.

I once said to my very dear, friend of fifty-plus years, "Carey, if you would have asked me thirty-two years ago where I thought we would be now, I never would have imagined battling life-threatening diseases such as my ancestors. We're not promised anything in life, in fact we're not even promised tomorrow. So, we embrace everyday as if it were our last!"

Today, we are still here, God willing. We know our journey will live on, even into our next lives. We are able to find such comfort in knowing this.

I'm also aware both he and I, along with our closely blended families and most all our siblings have found their eternal soulmates, and nothing makes us all happier. Together, they're all extremely strong, with full lives ahead of them. Such as my cousin Lisa, my aunt Marie's daughter, she and her husband David have together beautifully paved their lives' path of love and happiness.

I know this pleases my aunt as it truly means so much to her. They're extremely close, even living next door to one another for years! I feel good knowing they are there to keep an eye on one another as the years go by.

As a family we do need each other, often to pick one another up when we are down and to hold each other steady when we are shaken. We rely on our family's strength, showing and feeling love and compassion toward each other. So, in our family, strength is key. Strength gives us the will to keep going! I thank Noni for this. She was the strongest person besides my mother that I would know in my lifetime.

Chapter 6
SPIRITUAL GUIDANCE

This is the chapter that brings my book to life, as you will soon find out. It's also one of the main reasons behind the title of the book, *Book within a Book*.

What took place in my life for all of this to have happened was just short of several series of divine interventions from our higher forces. First, remember I lost my brother George in 1996, right after my father in 1995? Prior to losing brother George, who had relocated to Oregon, I had this vivid dream. I was in a hospital room in a building I had never been in. And in that dream, it was *not* familiar to me whatsoever, at least not yet. I saw Noni, Nane, my mother, and my father, all standing at this bedside. I woke from my sleep in a sweat, panicking, worried; I thought maybe this dream was to prepare me for my son in some way. Either way I felt something bad was going to happen to someone near and dear to me. A couple days later, I received a call from Wayne in Oregon. He was one of the reasons George moved there. They were very close growing up. But soon, I would learn his call was not a happy call. He called to tell me George was in a coma at the VA hospital, that I needed to get there as soon as I could. I dropped everything to head his way.

I arrived at the VA hospital only to find that it was the building in my dream. As we walked in, I knew I had been there before. It was quite eerie to say the least, but at the same time, I felt a huge relief now knowing the dream was not about my son after all. However, I knew exactly which way to go to reach that hospital room where my brother was from my dream. And sure enough, as I entered the room and stood in the very same spot I stood in my dream, chills ran up and down my entire body.

I knew at that very moment they were *all* standing there watching over George as I stared in their direction, letting them know I saw them, and I was aware this was serious! But at the same time, I was relieved they were there for him.

If all my family who had passed were all there, I needed to prepare myself for what would be coming next. The doctors called me and my husband, my boulder Erik, into a last-minute round-table meeting, telling us my big brother was brain-dead, and the machines were keeping him alive. I needed to give them permission to pull the plug. I was astonished to hear those words.

I said, *no way*! I could *not* make that decision nor give my permission! As far as I was concerned, there was *only* one person who can make that decision, and that was God himself. I went on to tell them I needed to be able to rest my head on my pillow at night, and bottom line, I would not be able to do so had I fulfilled their wish. With that, my husband and I got up from the table and excused ourselves from the meeting. We walked out of that room, never to speak to them again. Torn, knowing I couldn't do anything, that this was out of my control, we headed back to Florida, only to receive word that the doctors were stuck making the decision. In doing so, within two days my brother was gone from my world.

I now know the exact reason the family was there at his bedside, and that was to comfort him as they prepared to take him on his journey. For me, that ended up making his loss somewhat easier to try and accept, as they were now guiding me toward my grieving and healing journey.

As it turned out, some of us, more so than others in our family, are spiritually gifted. I believe it began with Noni at an extremely young age. Both my aunt Marie and I have some deeper spiritual abilities. Maybe this is where the saying "God will only give you what he thinks you can handle" comes from, especially with our enormous losses, one right after another.

Here's the other part of my book's inspiration, which was all prior to the spiritual story of George's passing.

We'll need to go back to December of 1987, six months after losing my precious mother and best friend, Lorraine. I had so many questions, one after another, that my mind could barely function. I desperately needed answers as to why my mother, my best friend, was taken from me at such a young age. She had only been in my world for the first thirty years of my life.

I found myself questioning God. What did I do to endure such pain and loss? One minute I was sad and a total wreck, then the next minute, I was mad. I found myself so mad at God at times, and I hated to be mad at him, but I was desperate for answers that weren't presenting themselves quickly enough for me.

The loss of her was so deeply devastating to me. I would have days of just crying my eyes out. I had no one to turn to who could understand the true depths of what I was experiencing. I felt so alone. People would say she was in a better place and time would heal my wound, but that's *not* what you want to tell someone in my shoes, *ever*! I needed answers to move forward, to begin the stages of properly grieving, followed by acceptance, and then finally, the healing process. If possible, I needed it desperately.

Suddenly I found myself heading to the bookstore, hopefully to find my answers. But first you need to know I was *not* an avid reader. In fact, most all my life, I may have read six books. So you, too, will find this story to be somewhat amazing.

I walked in the bookstore, feeling as though alarms should be sounding off because I couldn't tell you the last time I had been to a bookstore. But much to my amazement, *no* alarms sounded off. I was surprised and went forward, laser focused. I didn't know what I was looking for, so I just started looking at books. This one book literally jumped out at me. In fact, when I went to open it to read, it automatically opened to a page with a small paragraph, and as I read that paragraph, I knew my mother was speaking to me through that very paragraph.

You see, the book had several documented stories of people's near-death experiences and what happened on their journeys from people who had lived to talk about their journeys. I believe, in that paragraph, she was letting me know just what she herself had experienced in her own passing. As faith would have it, this happened to be one of my unanswered questions. I started to thumb through the book, and it captured my undivided attention in an odd way. I knew that I was meant to have it, as I felt it housed all the answers to all my questions. I purchased it immediately! This infamous book is called *Life After Life*, by Dr. Raymond Moody. To this very day, his book is my saving grace and will be forever!

This would be the catalyst for me to write my book, *Book within a Book*. Following the purchase of this amazing book, the next thing I knew, I was having yet another one of my vivid dreams, only to find out after reading more of my new book that these spurts of premonitions and vivid dreams weren't dreams at all. There is a chapter in the book called "Out of Body Experience," which was exactly what was happening to me, according to that chapter. My mother had come to me once again, and once again I thought it to be another dream. We found ourselves floating above my father's driveway. I remember that day like it was yesterday. It was daytime, and this was the last home my mother lived in before her journey.

By then, my father was in a new relationship after the loss of my mom, with a girl who had a young boy. As we floated above my dad's driveway, he pulled in, and out of the car stepped both Cathy and her young son Terry.

As we both were looking down at them, I would say hovering from approximately ten feet above, my mom asked me, "Who are they?"

I told her it was Cathy and her son Terry. I wanted her to know that I felt their relationship was OK, and she need not worry. I knew my mom very well, and if she thought I was OK with it, then she, too, would be OK with it as well.

I told my mother, "She's nice, and she makes Papa (my dad) happy, filling a void. Your loss has been tough on him."

I could tell my answer gave her comfort and satisfaction, and oddly enough in that moment, I found myself answering *her* question from beyond my world. Who would have ever guessed the questions would be reversed? We then found ourselves in the middle of my dad's yard, hovering this time about three or four feet off the ground, holding hands, going in circles like little girls do as best friends. Again, I'll never forget that moment either, as I hold it so near and dear to my heart to this day.

I asked her, "Are you OK? Where have you been for the last six months? I have been so worried about you and missed you terribly."

She lovingly replied to me, "I'm just fine, and you do not need to worry about me, I'll be OK." I did find comfort in her words and was able to understand life a little better then, knowing she *is* OK. Plus, my very own mother had just given me the answer to one of my biggest questions connected to the loss of her, for which I had desperately searched.

In that moment I felt a deep connection to God as well. I knew he was coming forward for me, totally aware of the darkness I had endured.

I went on to read that entire book, *Life After Life*, and the more I read it, the better and better I felt. It was clearly heaven-sent to me through my mom. I tell everyone who has suffered the loss of a loved one to get the book. It will help! Since my edition was from 1987, I tell people it may have changed and to just be aware.

THE BOOK WITHIN A BOOK

One day at work, in the year 2006, my colleague's mother had lost her husband of sixty years. She was devastated, as you can imagine, so I lent her my book for her mother to find comfort. I told her to take as long as she would need to read it, and when she was done, I would get it back. Months went by, and the next thing I knew, my colleague told me, "Mom did something with your book. She could not find it, for the life of her." She was frantically apologizing over and over to me, knowing how near and dear the book was to me. I told her not to worry, if it helped her mother like it did me, then I did my job! But deep down inside, I was crushed.

It was my connection to my mother, my best friend. The thought of losing that precious connection was devastating, to say the least. Understand, I loaned the book to her in 2006, while living in Florida. I had the book since 1987. I needed to try and move on, and in doing so, I lost contact with my old colleague.

Life did go on, and we ended up relocating across the states to Oregon in 2014. Meanwhile, I did get a newer version of that very book, and just like I said, I would later pass it on. I was really trying to achieve that reconnection to my mother again. Then one day in 2019, literally years later, I walked to my mailbox, and there was a mysterious package. When I opened the package, low and behold was my 1987 *Life after Life* book, with a sweet little note saying, "I hope this is the Debra I worked with back in 2006, in Florida. I hope the book has made it back home to you!"

Immediately, tears filled my eyes. Chills ran up and down my entire body. This can't be! *All* these years later, across miles and miles, it was basically chalked up as a huge loss of thirteen years since I last saw it. Here it was, once again before my very own eyes, in the very hands that embraced it all those years ago, thirty-seven to be exact. I looked up to the heavens above and said, "You're home once again, Mom. Boy, how I've truly missed you. You've no idea. I promise to *never ever* let you out of sight, ever again!"

The book will remain in my possession for the rest of my life! If this isn't a clear case of spiritual divine intervention in motion, then clearly, I don't know what is or would be.

Going back to that *aha!* moment in the earlier chapter of my book, when I wrote of the two women giving birth to their babies from that band member at the same time:

I'm a firm believer there are *no* coincidences in life, especially knowing there are three hundred sixty-five days in a year, as well as twenty-four hours per day. In that very moment, on that very day, I believe a clear message surfaced from a much higher power as well! This was indeed the work of our Heavenly Father, letting this man know he was carefully being watched from above, that he would endure his day of reckoning one day, and to be prepared!

Going back to the loss of Nane, my mother's mother back in 1996. If you remember, I wrote of her funeral and how her wake was on my mother's exact birthday nine years after losing my mother. Again, I felt as though we were being presented with yet another clear message from our higher-ups. What I took from this day came to me so crystal clear, and as I embraced it close to my heart, I remember at this point I had read my *Life After Life* book several times over again. The message perceived on this sad day turned out to be a life-altering moment because what started as a deeply sad day ended up becoming a happy, glorious day of celebration.

THE BOOK WITHIN A BOOK

You see, since this step of the burial was happening on my mother's birthday, my mother was letting us all know she has her mother with her, and together they will begin the journey!

I pray to my God as well as my angels and spirit guides daily as they watch over me and everyone I love. I thank God for guiding me to the book *Life After Life* and for Dr. Raymond Moody all those years ago. I thank God for bringing the book back home to me through my mom all those years later. I go on to cherish all the related connections to it.

God is good! Believe in your heart, never doubting it for one second. He'll always be there for you! Life is good!

Special thanks go out to Dr. Raymond Moody for his research and the creation of his amazing book! I could not have done it without it and will not do without it. It's had such an impact on my life. And thanks to his amazing book. I know in my heart *Life After Life* is good too!

When I find myself today trying to comfort someone walking in the very shoes I had worn thirty-seven years ago, I simply give them a copy of that book, knowing its amazing powers. Because I can honestly say from my heart, they are the only words you want to hear when faced with such loss.

Bless all who read my book! And many thanks to you for welcoming us into your homes. I really hope you too find peace, happiness, spiritual guidance, as well as some much-needed answers through my life experiences shared in this book.

God bless!

ABOUT THE AUTHOR

Debra Steele was born in 1956 in Massachusetts. Her hobbies include art, music, cooking, baking, and spending time with her family. She loves animals, especially deer and horses. Some people even refer to her as the "deer whisperer." Professionally, she attended some college courses in the medical field and managed a doctor's office for several years. Helping people is her passion. She has been known to give dinner to the homeless on a whim. *The Book within a Book* is her first book, and she hopes her journey touches those who read it.

www.ingramcontent.com/pod-product-compliance
Lightning Source LLC
LaVergne TN
LVHW051922060526
838201LV00060B/4137